Author:
Jacqueline Morley studied English literature at Oxford University. She has taught English and history and now works as a freelance writer. She has written historical fiction and non-fiction for children.

Artist:
David Antram was born in Brighton, England, in 1958. He studied at Eastbourne College of Art and then worked in advertising for 15 years before becoming a full-time artist. He has illustrated many children's non-fiction books.

Series creator:
David Salariya was born in Dundee, Scotland. He has illustrated a wide range of books and has created and designed many new series for publishers in the UK and overseas. David established The Salariya Book Company in 1989. He lives in Brighton with his wife, illustrator Shirley Willis, and their son Jonathan.

Editor: Stephen Haynes

Editorial Assistant: Mark Williams

Visit
www.salariya.com
for our online catalogue and **free** interactive web books.

Published in Great Britain in MMXIV by
Book House, an imprint of
The Salariya Book Company Ltd
25 Marlborough Place, Brighton BN1 1UB
www.salariya.com
www.book-house.co.uk

HB ISBN-13: 978-1-908973-77-1
PB ISBN-13: 978-1-908973-78-8

1 3 5 7 9 8 6 4 2

A CIP catalogue record for this book is available from the British Library.

Printed and bound in China.

Visit our website at **www.book-house.co.uk**
or go to **www.salariya.com** for **free** electronic versions of:
You Wouldn't Want to be an Egyptian Mummy!
You Wouldn't Want to be a Roman Gladiator!
You Wouldn't Want to be a Polar Explorer!
You Wouldn't Want to sail on a 19th-Century Whaling Ship!

PAPER FROM SUSTAINABLE FORESTS

Avoid being Leonardo da Vinci!

Written by
Jacqueline Morley

Illustrated by
David Antram

Created and designed by
David Salariya

The Danger Zone™

Contents

Introduction

Florence in the 1460s is a great place to be: the liveliest of the city-states that make up a very disunited Italy. It's buzzing with ideas. Scholars have been rediscovering the arts of ancient Greece and Rome, and that has produced new ways of writing and of depicting the world. And Florence has the sort of brilliant craftsmen – sculptors, painters and metalworkers – who can put these ideas into practice. You're apprenticed to one, the painter and goldsmith Andrea Verrocchio. His workshop is the best in town.

One day, in 1466, a new apprentice arrives. His name is Leonardo and he's unlike anyone you've met. He's a brilliant artist and a great companion, but he can suddenly become withdrawn and turn away from people. Yet he's tender-hearted: you've seen him buying caged birds just to set them free. He's going to make a difference to your life!

LEONARDO was born in 1452 at a farmhouse near the town of Vinci, about 25 km west of Florence.

In Verrochio's workshop

You well remember Leonardo's arrival. At nearly 15 he was quite old to be starting an apprenticeship. Most boys begin at 12, as you did, for it takes many years to master all the crafts of Verrocchio's studio. The master supplies portraits, gilded altarpieces, sculptures in terracotta, marble or bronze, gold and silver ware, and painted decorations of all kinds. And he's an engineer too! You can see he's impressed by those drawings that Leonardo's father is showing him. They must be unusually good!

That's all his own work, you know.

An apprentice's tasks

Quill

To make your own brushes, tuck weasel hairs in one end of a hollow quill, and a handle in the other.

MAKING PIGMENTS. Grind up coloured earths or rocks, then mix with egg yolk or oil to make them flow.

LEARN TO DRAW by copying the best works, especially the antique Roman ones that are being excavated now.

Leonardo shows promise

LEONARDO'S FATHER, Master Piero da Vinci, gets him to restore an old shield that a peasant wants mended. By tacking together bits of various ugly dead creatures, Leonardo creates a monster.

HE PAINTS IT on the shield. Lit by a spotlight in a dark corner, it terrifies his father. Impressed, his father sells it for a high price and fobs the peasant off with another shield.

An outstanding apprentice

Turning his hand to anything

A FULLY TRAINED APPRENTICE can turn out objects in bronze or precious metals; sacred pictures and portraits; sets and costumes for pageants and celebrations; painted decorations on furniture, banners and shields – whatever a patron demands.

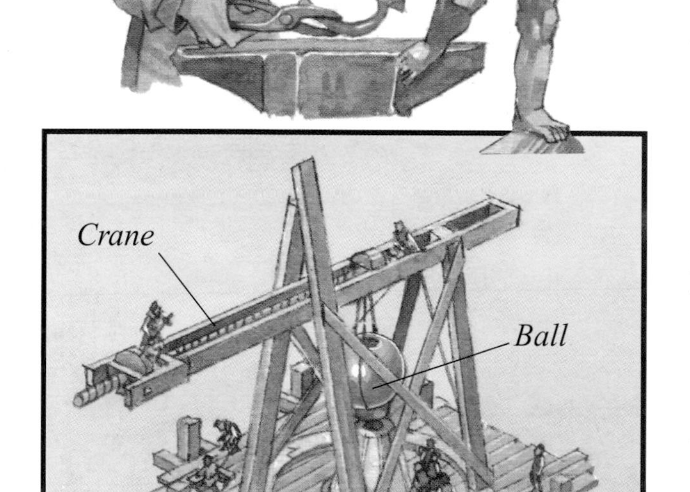

After years spent mastering drawing, pupils at last get to use paint. You're not good enough yet to do the background details in Verrocchio's work, but Leonardo is doing foreground figures already. The master says he couldn't do them better himself.

Verrochio is now working on a major goldsmithing commission: a gilded copper ball, 2.5 metres wide and weighing over 20 tonnes, for the top of the cathedral dome. Leonardo is fascinated by the engineering involved in getting it up there. He says art and science depend upon each other.

The great copper ball (1469)

THE DOME of Florence Cathedral is still quite new: the decorative lantern on the top was finished only a few years ago, in 1461. The architect, Filippo Brunelleschi, created special hoists and cranes to lift the copper ball into place. But he didn't live to finish the job, so Verrocchio is now using his machines. Leonardo is studying them closely.

Handy hint
Don't expect your best efforts to win you fame. No work is signed by the artist – it all goes out under the studio owner's name.
This'll knock their socks off.

Going it alone

When Leonardo sets up his own studio and offers you a job, you jump at it. With friends who drop in, talk a lot and make music, the studio's a lively place – except when Leonardo shuts himself away and scribbles non-stop in his notebooks. He seems keener on these than on his painting. He'll spend ages on the design and underpainting of a job, then lose interest and not finish it. An *Adoration of the Magi*, begun in 1481, is making no progress at all. The friars who ordered it are complaining.

Preparing a panel painting

A DRAWING on paper (the 'cartoon') is attached to a prepared wooden panel and its outlines are marked with pin-pricks. When charcoal is rubbed through these, and the cartoon lifted away, the design appears on the panel as a series of dots (1). Next comes the underpainting, in tones of brown or grey – darker for shadows, lighter for highlights (2).

Handy hint

If you like to make lots of subtle changes as you paint, mix your colours with oil. Old-fashioned egg-tempera is fast-drying and can't be fiddled with.

THE UNDERPAINTING gives roundness to the forms. Colour is added last (3), in semi-transparent glazes (layers of paint thinned with oil).

THE FRIARS aren't paying in advance, so Leonardo is very hard up. He has to borrow money from them to buy colours. For doing odd jobs (such as mending the monastery clock) they pay him in firewood.

LEAVING TOWN. In 1481 the Pope asks Lorenzo de' Medici (left), Florence's top man, to send him the town's best artists to decorate the Sistine Chapel in Rome. Leonardo, who is getting a reputation for unreliability, is not among the chosen. He feels he's not valued in Florence. He decides to leave.

In Milan

Milan's ruthless ruler, Duke Ludovico Sforza

You've followed Leonardo to Milan, where he's hoping for work at the ducal court. So far he's got none. Luckily, in 1483 a religious confraternity employs him to paint an altarpiece. They're expecting the usual Madonna and angels with gilded haloes. When the work's delivered (two years late), it shows realistic figures among dark rocks, and only one angel – with no halo! The confraternity are disgusted and won't pay. Leonardo now has a lawsuit on his hands.

Working for the duke

DUKE LUDOVICO first employs Leonardo as a musician, playing the lira da braccio and singing to the lute. Soon he is organising court entertainments.

AT LAST, Ludovico orders a portrait – of his mistress, lovely Cecilia Gallerani. Leonardo shows her with an ermine, a Sforza symbol.

LEONARDO creates amazing stage effects. One shows a golden world with shimmering stars and figures representing planets.

Handy hint

From Leonardo's ideal city: spiral staircases to stop people peeing in corners of landings.

Plague in Milan

IN 1484 the dreaded plague (above) strikes Milan. It lasts for three years. Leonardo believes it is caused by crowded, dirty living conditions. He tackles the problem scientifically. To prevent plague he designs a healthy city (below), open, airy, and watered by canals. It is never built.

Verrochio's statue of Bartolomeo Colleoni

A really big project

udovico is getting Leonardo to make a huge bronze statue to commemorate the duke's father. He is to be shown mounted, and Leonardo's clay model for the horse is now on show. Casting something so enormous is an exciting challenge for him. He's stockpiled 70 tonnes of bronze. But in 1494 the duke takes the bronze to make cannon to fight the French – a cruel disappointment!

IT'S TRADITIONAL to commemorate a leader by showing him looking impressive on horseback.

LEONARDO'S FIRST PLAN (right) was for a rearing horse, but he realised that the hind legs alone would not be strong enough to support a three-times life-size statue.

Casting a bronze statue

LEONARDO has spent years, on and off, on the problem of casting the horse. Using the traditional technique, he'd need a huge casting pit and four vast furnaces to keep so much bronze at melting point.

Handy hint

Keep everything dry. Any damp in the mould can cause an explosion which will shower you with white-hot metal.

TO MAKE a bronze cast: first the wax or clay model is split into sections (1) and a two-part clay cast is taken of each section (2).

1

2

THE TWO PARTS of each cast are joined (3), to make hollow moulds of the original sections.

4

HOT WAX is poured in (4) and swirled around to coat the inside of the mould. The wax will harden to provide hollow replicas of the original sections.

3

Join

THE WAX FIGURE is now encased in heat-resistant plaster (6) and heated till the wax melts and runs out at the base. This leaves an empty space exactly the shape of the original model, but hollow.

THE WAX SECTIONS are joined to form a hollow version of the whole figure (5). It is given a solid core of plaster, and wax rods are added. They will become ducts (tubes) to let the molten bronze flow in.

5

Wax rods

7

MOLTEN BRONZE from the furnace is poured into the mould (7). It flows through the tubes until every hollow is filled. When the bronze cools the plaster is chipped away (8), the ducts (now bronze) are sawn off, and surface details are chiselled and polished (9).

8

The *Last Supper*

In 1495 Leonardo is commissioned to decorate a wall in the dining hall of a Dominican monastery. The subject is Christ's last meal with his disciples – a suitable choice for a dining room.

Two years later he's still working on it. He wants every figure, every face, every gesture to be just right. This involves long periods of thought and endless retouchings. The prior keeps complaining about the delay. Leonardo tells him if he doesn't shut up he'll use his face for Judas. That makes Ludovico laugh.

ON SOME DAYS Leonardo paints from dawn to dusk non-stop. You put out his lunch – he doesn't touch it. On others he does nothing but gaze at his work for hours on end, completely lost in thought.

WALL PAINTINGS are usually done on wet plaster, so the colour bonds with the wall plaster. To allow for constant alterations, Leonardo's painting on dry plaster instead, with a mix of his own invention: egg-tempera and oil. Who knows whether it will last?

EACH MORNING and evening he wanders through the roughest parts of the city, searching for a truly evil face for Judas.

HE'S WORRIED about the picture surface. It seems flaky in places. The wall behind is damp, which doesn't help.

Handy hint

Damp walls have their uses. Leonardo says that damp stains can give an artist design ideas.

THE DUKE is a stingy patron. Payments often don't arrive. Leonardo pens a polite complaint: 'If Your Lordship thought I had money, Your Lordship was deceived.'

The great inventor

hen Ludovico has to flee the invading French, Leonardo is without a patron. In 1502 he finds work with scheming prince Cesare Borgia, who wants his advice on making war machines. Mechanical problems fascinate Leonardo. His super-brain explores all kinds of science: physics, mathematics, chemistry, anatomy, architecture, hydraulics, aerodynamics, optics – his study is littered with papers and notebooks filled with his observations, designs and experiments.

Leonardo is left-handed, and he writes his notes from right to left.

Weapons of war

IT'S NOT THE KILLING that Leonardo's keen on, but the thrill of putting his scientific theories into practice. He designs a steam-powered cannon (below right) centuries before the invention of the steam engine.

His scheme for a tank (below). The cutaway interior view shows big crank-handles, turned by hand, that cause gearwheels to engage with the main wheels.

A modern drawing of Leonardo's steam cannon; it was never built for real.

Leonardo's plans for a helicopter and a parachute

Flight: a lifelong dream

THE IDEA of a flying machine has obsessed Leonardo for years. He's studied the structure of birds' wings and designed lots of machines that try to imitate it. He'd like someone to do a trial take-off from the roof. Not you, you hope!

SADLY, these flying machines could never have worked. People are much heavier than birds, and human chest muscles just aren't strong enough to work the wings.

The anatomist

LEONARDO believes the human body reflects the workings of the universe. This drawing, 'Vitruvian Man', shows how the proportions of the human figure follow the rules of geometry, as set out by the ancient Roman architect Vitruvius.

Leonardo says you'll never draw the human figure well unless you know which bits do what and how they hang together. Other artists study muscles from the outside, but he wants to know what goes on inside. There's only one way to find out – cut a corpse open and take a look. You can't do this without a licence, and many people are opposed to it. They think it's prying into God's secrets, or dabbling in black magic. In 1515 an ill-wisher reports him to the Pope.

LEONARDO has been making cross-sections of the skull. He hopes to be able to pinpoint the exact spot where consciousness is located.

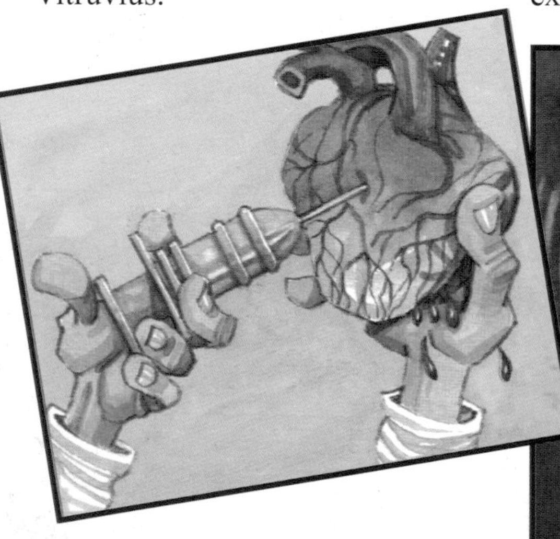

WHENEVER a local hospital is able to supply a body, Leonardo studies every organ closely. He cuts it out, washes it and injects it with melted wax to preserve its living shape. He draws it from every angle and makes pages and pages of notes.

TO SEE exactly how muscles and tendons work together, he replaces arm and leg muscles with lengths of string and tugs them.

WHEN HE'S LUCKY ENOUGH to get a body, he won't stop work until the smell is unbearable. Often he works all night.

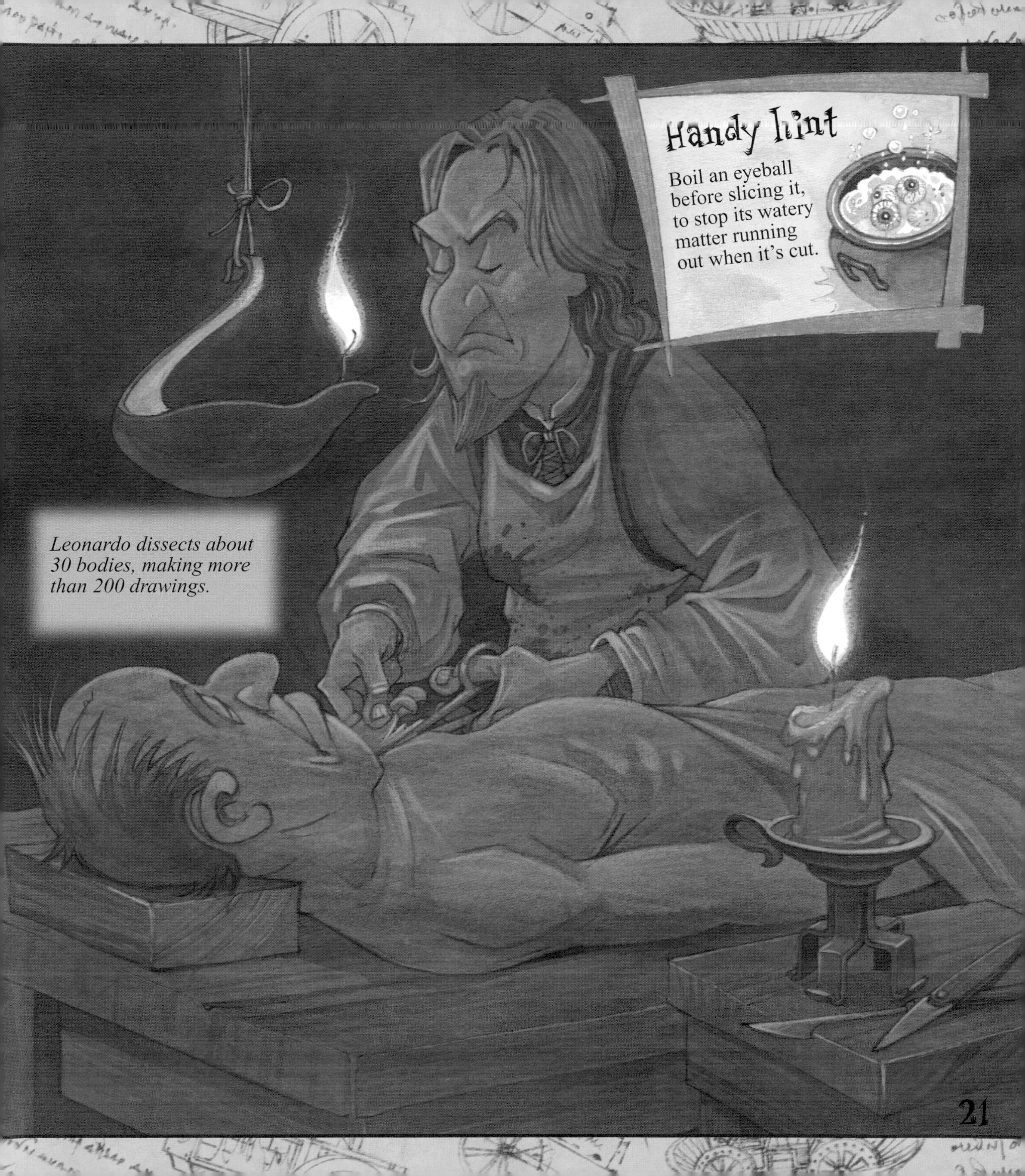

Leonardo dissects about 30 bodies, making more than 200 drawings.

The battle of the battles

Back in Florence, in 1502, Leonardo gets a big commission: to paint a wall of the city's Council Hall with a vast battle scene. The job's giving him a lot of stress, especially since his rival, Michelangelo, is doing another battle on the opposite wall. They don't see eye to eye on art. Leonardo thinks Michelangelo's figures are too muscular (like bunches of radishes, he's said). Michelangelo says Leonardo starts big projects he can't finish. He taunts him publicly (and most unfairly) about the giant horse he didn't cast.

Some Florentine citizens are arguing about the meaning of a famous poem...

Here's Michelangelo – he'll explain it to you.

THE PAINTING will be vast – 18 m long and over 7 m high. Leonardo has invented a mobile, screw-adjusted scaffold to get him where he needs to be.

THINGS GO WRONG right from the start. A dreadful storm breaks out. A howling wind tears through a window, ripping the cartoon away and spilling a pail of water down the wall.

LEONARDO's experimental ways with paint are causing problems. The colours aren't drying fast enough. Paint at the top is running down the walls.

THE COUNCILLORS are muttering that they're not getting value for money. Leonardo's salary is paid to him all in small change. He refuses it, saying: 'I am no penny painter.'

Mona Lisa

Leonardo is working on a portrait that is said by everyone to be a wonder, though you can't really say why. He's spent four years on it already, on and off. It's not of anyone special, just a well-to-do housewife, Mona Lisa, wife of a Florentine silk merchant. (*Mona* is short for *Madonna* or 'My Lady'.) Yet there is something about it that fascinates everyone. Perhaps it's the slight smile on her lips, or the mysterious mountain background which seems almost to dissolve in a soft, smoky light.

Leonardo prefers to paint his sitters in the early evening. At that time of day shadows are softest and objects are bathed in a gentle light. Shadow and light are the most important things to capture, he says, because it's through them that the shapes of objects are revealed to us.

LEONARDO spends as much or possibly even more time criticising his work than getting on with it. He is never satisfied that he has caught the effect he's after. He makes countless tiny additions and alterations with brushstrokes so fine they're invisible.

POOR MONA LISA poses day after day. They say that to stop her looking glum Leonardo hires musicians and clowns to entertain her. He'll do anything to get the look he wants.

MONA LISA'S HUSBAND never gets the portrait he commissioned. Leonardo keeps saying it's not finished and will not part with it. He keeps the picture with him till his dying day.

Handy hint
Leonardo says:
To make a fine
green, mix the
pigment with
bitumen. This will
make the shadows
darker.

A guest of the King

When Leonardo revisits Milan (to deal with that long-running lawsuit over the Madonna), King Louis XII of France, who has now become ruler of Milan as well, insists he should stay and work for him. The French appreciate Leonardo's genius more than the Italians. Louis is all set to take the *Last Supper* to Paris, till someone mentions it is painted on a wall. In 1516 Louis's successor, Francis I, offers Leonardo a permanent home in France.

THANKS to Francis I's kindness, Leonardo (now elderly, as this self-portrait shows) finds a quiet haven at the manor house of Cloux near Amboise.

Worries and disappointments

THE POPE has second thoughts about a painting he's commissioned when he hears Leonardo is experimenting with final varnishes before he's even started painting.

IN 1504 Leonardo's father and his much-loved uncle die, leading to sordid legal wrangles with relatives over the two wills.

HE'S TRYING to sort his huge mass of notes according to subject, to form them into treatises – a mammoth task.

Leonardo and Francis at Cloux

Security at last

FRANCIS enjoys discussing a vast range of topics with Leonardo. He says there can be no-one in the world who knows more of art and philosophy than he does.

LEONARDO DIES in 1519 – in the king's arms, it's said. You weren't there, so you can't be sure. Francis was supposed to be away signing a treaty, but perhaps he got someone else to do that for him.

Leonardo now

The Mona Lisa *is displayed behind bulletproof glass at the Louvre Museum, Paris.*

Nowadays Leonardo is rated a super-genius of art. Crowds throng to see the *Mona Lisa*, the most famous painting in the world. But, just as importantly, he was a scientist far ahead of his time, rejecting the old idea that knowledge is contained in the wisdom of the past. He believed it is expanded through observation of the outside world, and through testing one's observations by experiment. This is now accepted as the only valid method of scientific research.

TRAGICALLY FEW of Leonardo's works – paintings, drawings or notebooks – survive. His giant clay horse was used for target practice by French soldiers and finally crumbled to nothing.

WHEN THE CHURCH where he was buried was demolished, its skeletons were dumped in a common grave. In 1863 the skeleton with the biggest skull was randomly claimed as his.

HIS GREAT WALL PAINTINGS became disaster areas because of his experiments with paint. The *Last Supper* almost flaked away – much of what we see now is the work of restorers.

Handy hint

If you find a faded drawing with notes written right to left, take a careful look. You never know your luck!

LEONARDO left his notebooks to a pupil, whose son inherited them and thought them worthless. He chopped bits out to sell as individual drawings, or just gave pages away.

THOSE PAPERS that survive are almost beyond price. Computer magnate Bill Gates paid $30,800,000 for some in 1994.

TRUSTING LEONARDO'S SCIENCE. On 26 June 2000 British skydiver Adrian Nicholas made a successful descent over Kruger National Park using a parachute made exactly to Leonardo's design.

Glossary

aerodynamics The scientific study of the movements of air, and of objects moving through air.

altarpiece A painting or sculpture displayed on the altar of a church.

anatomy The scientific study of the bodily structure of humans, animals and other living organisms.

apprentice A young person who works for an employer in return for training.

apprenticeship The position that an apprentice takes.

bitumen A sticky, black, tar-like substance found in the ground. Diluted with oil, it was sometimes added to colours to produce darker tones.

bronze A mixture of copper and (usually) tin, which can be cast to make statues.

cartoon A drawing on paper which is the final, full-scale design for a painting.

cast To make an object by pouring liquid material into a mould.

city-state A self-governing state consisting of a city and its surrounding territory. In Leonardo's time, much of Italy consisted of city-states which were often at war with one another.

confraternity A society which performs religious or charitable works.

crank-handle A rod with a right-angled bend in it, which is turned to set other machine parts in motion.

dissect To cut up a body or organ in order to study what is inside.

Dominican Belonging to the order of friars founded in the 13th century by St Dominic.

duct A tube to convey liquid or gas to where it is needed.

egg-tempera A fast-drying and long-lasting paint made from pigment mixed with egg yolk.

friar A member of a religious order which depends on charity.

hydraulics The scientific study of the movement of water.

lira da braccio A 7-stringed musical instrument which resembles the viola.

lute A guitar-like instrument with a pear-shaped body.

Madonna The Italian word for 'My Lady'. It is often used as a title for the Virgin Mary.

Magi Another name for the Three Kings or Three Wise Men who visited the infant Jesus.

master A skilled craftsman who has passed an examination and is allowed to train apprentices.

optics The scientific study of the properties of light.

patron A person who gives regular employment to an artist.

pigment Any kind of colouring matter which can be ground into a powder and mixed with a medium (egg, oil, etc.) to make paint.

plague An infectious, usually fatal disease, spread by fleas carried by rats.

Pope The head of the Roman Catholic Church.

prior The head of certain religious houses, such as a Dominican convent.

quill The tubular part of a bird's feather, by which it is attached to the bird's skin.

terracotta Pottery made from a brownish-red clay.

treatise A piece of scholarly writing on a particular subject; a textbook.

treaty A peace agreement between two countries or states.

wineskin A large leather bag for carrying wine.

Index

Note: Titles of Leonardo's paintings are in italics.